Scrap Rat

Written by Clare Helen Welsh

Illustrated by Irene Montano

Collins

Stan has some card and some pens.

Snip!

2

Stan has a pot and some clips.

Stick!

Scrap Rat runs to the sink.
Stan yells, "Stop rat!"

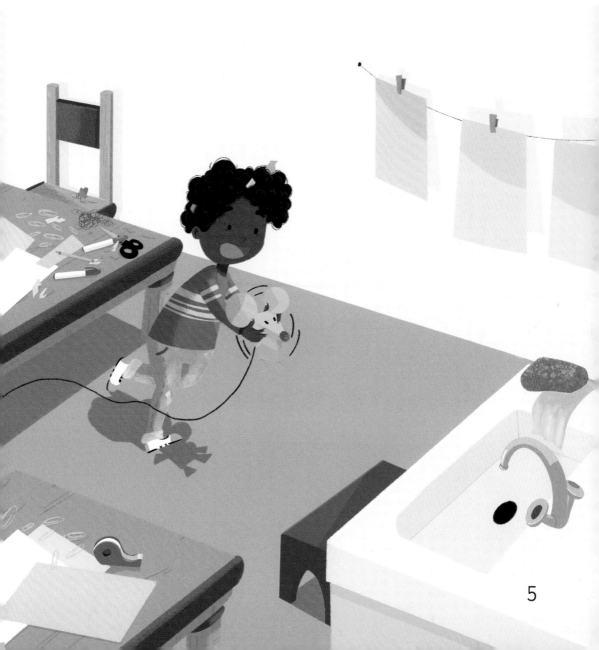

Scrap Rat runs on. His ear comes off.

Scrap Rat jumps in the sandpit.
Fliss yells, "Stop rat!"

Scrap Rat jumps high. His tail comes off.

Scrap Rat runs into Wilf the cat.

Scrap Rat is torn!
Stan has a plan.

He gets pens, clips, card and a pot.

Scrap Rat has his ears and tail back!

Wilf the cat is back too ...

Stop, cat!

Stan map

After reading

Letters and Sounds: Phase 4

Word count: 102

Focus on adjacent consonants with short vowel phonemes, e.g. s/c/r/a/p

Common exception words: some, comes, to, the, into, he

Curriculum links (EYFS): Expressive Arts and Design: Exploring and using media and materials

Curriculum links (National Curriculum, Year 1): PSHE; Art and Design

Early learning goals: Reading: use phonic knowledge to decode regular words and read them aloud accurately; demonstrate understanding when talking with others about what they have read

National Curriculum learning objectives: Reading/word reading: apply phonic knowledge and skills as the route to decode words; read accurately by blending sounds in unfamiliar words containing GPCs that have been taught; read other words of more than one syllable that contain taught GPCs; read aloud accurately books that are consistent with their developing phonic knowledge; re-read books to build up their fluency and confidence in word reading; Reading/comprehension: link what they have read or hear read to their own experiences; discuss word meanings; discuss the significance of the title and events

Developing fluency

- Your child may enjoy listening to you read the book.
- Look at page 4 together. Model using expression and a voice to read the speech bubble. Talk about how we might read sentences with exclamation marks.
- Now look at pages 12 and 13. Ask your child if they can see any exclamation marks. Read the main text on pages 12 and 13 and ask your child to read the speech bubble.

Phonic practice

- Practise reading words that contain adjacent consonants. Look through the book. What words can your child find that begin with "st"? (*Stan, stick, stop*)

Extending vocabulary

- Ask your child:
  - Scrap rat **jumps**. Can you think of another word for jumps? (e.g. *leaps, bounces, hops*)
  - Stan uses the scissors to **snip** the paper. Can you think of another word for snip? (e.g. *cut, trim, slice*)